ALL AROUND THE WORLD
JAPAN

by Jessica Dean

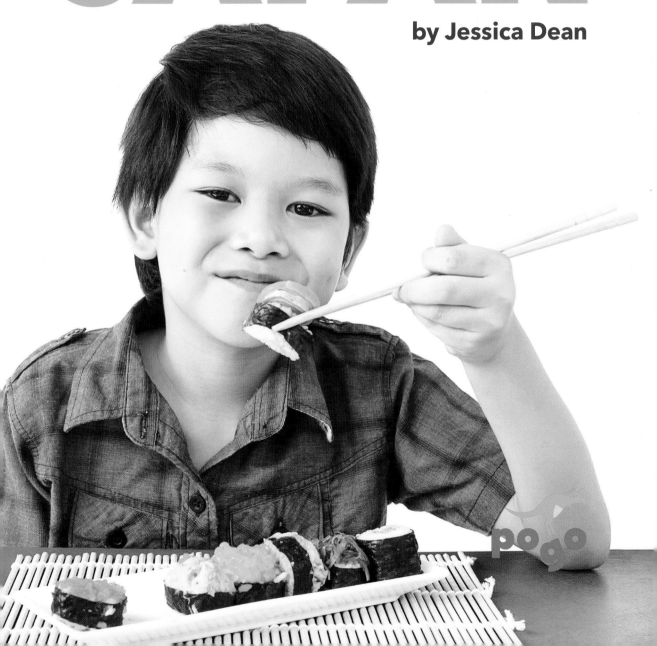

pogo

Ideas for Parents and Teachers

Pogo Books let children practice reading informational text while introducing them to nonfiction features such as headings, labels, sidebars, maps, and diagrams, as well as a table of contents, glossary, and index.

Carefully leveled text with a strong photo match offers early fluent readers the support they need to succeed.

Before Reading

• "Walk" through the book and point out the various nonfiction features. Ask the student what purpose each feature serves.

• Look at the glossary together. Read and discuss the words.

Read the Book

• Have the child read the book independently.

• Invite him or her to list questions that arise from reading.

After Reading

• Discuss the child's questions. Talk about how he or she might find answers to those questions.

• Prompt the child to think more. Ask: Japan's cities are very crowded. Do you live in a crowded city or an area with a low population?

Pogo Books are published by Jump!
5357 Penn Avenue South
Minneapolis, MN 55419
www.jumplibrary.com

Library of Congress Cataloging-in-Publication Data

Names: Dean, Jessica, 1963- author.
Title: Japan / by Jessica Dean.
Description: Pogo Books. | Minneapolis, MN: Jump!, Inc., 2018. | Series: All around the world
Includes index. | Audience: Ages 7-10.
Identifiers: LCCN 2017055819 (print)
LCCN 2017057001 (ebook)
ISBN 9781624969164 (hardcover: alk. paper)
ISBN 9781624969171 (pbk.)
ISBN 9781624969188 (ebook)
Subjects: LCSH: Japan—Juvenile literature.
Classification: LCC DS806 .D362 2018 (print)
LCC DS806 (ebook) | DDC 952—dc23
LC record available at https://lccn.loc.gov/2017055819

Editor: Kristine Spanier
Book Designer: Michelle Sonnek

Photo Credits: kuriaki1/Shutterstock, cover; Pair Srinrat/Shutterstock, 1; Pixfiction/Shutterstock, 3; Takashi Images/Shutterstock, 4; prasit chansarekorn/iStock, 5; Ondrej Prosicky/Shutterstock, 6-7; Yupgi/Shutterstock, 8-9; Moolkum/Shutterstock, 10; Bloomberg/Getty, 11; TommL/iStock, 12-13; Tom Wang/Shutterstock, 14-15; takayuki/Shutterstock, 16; Manfred Rutz/Getty, 17; Ryzhkov Photography/Shutterstock, 18-19; Bobo Ling/Shutterstock, 20-21; prapass/Shutterstock, 23.

Printed in the United States of America at Corporate Graphics in North Mankato, Minnesota.

TABLE OF CONTENTS

CHAPTER 1

WELCOME TO JAPAN!

Blooming cherry blossoms. Cities packed with people. Beautiful beaches. Mountains capped with snow. These are all sights found in Japan!

cherry blossoms

Mount Fuji

Japan is a chain of islands off the eastern coast of Asia. Mount Fuji stands near Tokyo. It is the tallest mountain here.

red-crowned
crane

Forests spread across the land. Snow monkeys chatter in the trees. Bears, foxes, and deer search for food. Red-crowned cranes can be found in **marshes**. Pairs dance together.

DID YOU KNOW?

Red-crowned cranes are a sign of good luck. These birds are often shown in Japanese art. They are even on the money!

Tall castles are found in Japan. Some were built more than 1,000 years ago! They were built along **trade** routes and rivers. Why? To defend those areas.

From the outside, a castle might appear to have three to five stories. But the inside has more levels. Why? To confuse **invaders**.

Himeji
Castle

CHAPTER 2

BUSY AND CROWDED

Most of Japan's cities lie along the coasts. High-rise apartments are common. City gardens are filled with bonsai. They are tiny trees trimmed into special shapes.

bonsai

Many people work in **service jobs** like banking. Factory workers build cars. Machinery. Even fun toys!

Tokyo

Tokyo is the **capital**. It has more people than many countries do! There is always a traffic jam. Most people take trains or the **subway** to get around.

The **prime minister** runs the government. Japan's **emperor** attends special events.

Japanese students study very hard. They wear school uniforms. Children bow to teachers. Some attend juku, or **cram** schools, for more studies after school.

Children take turns cleaning the school. It is the duty of all students to help. Then they practice sports or music. Or they create art.

The Japanese language has three alphabets. Kanji is for ideas, words, or names. Hiragana is used for other words from Japan. Katakana is for words from other languages.

kanji examples

fire

friend

brave

hiragana examples

え

e

た

ta

よ

yo

katakana examples

o

ka

マ

ma

CHAPTER 3

LIFE IN JAPAN

The kimono is the traditional robe that has been worn for hundreds of years. It is held in place by an obi. These robes are now worn for **ceremonies** and special events.

obi ·····▶

kimono ·····▶

Men's kimonos are simpler. They come in colors like black, gray, brown, or blue.

Vegetables and fish are part of most dishes. Rice is served at every meal. Noodles are made from rice flour. Rice cakes with sweet filling are served for dessert.

When soup is served, chopsticks are used to eat the vegetables and noodles. Then people slurp up the broth. Tea is served in small cups.

WHAT DO YOU THINK?

Fish is eaten often in Japan. Given the country's location, why do you think fish is a part of most meals?

chopsticks

origami

The people here like to go to baseball games. They play soccer. People of all ages fold thin paper into animals or other shapes. This is called **origami**.

Children's Day is a special holiday. It is on May 5. Families voice hopes for when their children are grown. In spring, the cherry blossoms bloom. People picnic together under the trees.

What would you like to do in Japan?

DID YOU KNOW?

Japanese comics are called manga. Film and television animation is called anime.

QUICK FACTS & TOOLS

JAPAN

Location: Eastern Asia

Size: 145,914 square miles (377,915 square kilometers)

Population: 126,451,398 (July 2017 estimate)

Capital: Tokyo

Type of Government: parliamentary constitutional monarchy

Language: Japanese

Exports: cars, car parts, iron and steel products, plastic materials

GLOSSARY

capital: A city where government leaders meet.

ceremonies: Formal events that mark important occasions.

cram: To study very hard over a short period of time.

emperor: The ruler of an empire.

invaders: People who enter an area for conquest or plunder.

marshes: Areas of wet, muddy land.

origami: The Japanese art of folding paper into decorative shapes.

prime minister: The leader of a country.

service jobs: Jobs and work that provide services for others, such as hotel, restaurant, and retail positions.

subway: Train that runs on underground tracks.

trade: The business of buying and selling goods.

INDEX

TO LEARN MORE

Learning more is as easy as 1, 2, 3.

1) Go to www.factsurfer.com

2) Enter "Japan" into the search box.

3) Click the "Surf" button to see a list of websites.

With factsurfer, finding more information is just a click away.